CONTENTS

Above
The Imperial War Museum.

Above right
Robert Crawford, Director General of the Imperial War Museum.

Front cover
Front view of the Museum showing the 15-inch guns from HMS Resolution (left) and HMS Ramillies (right).

Back cover
Pale Armistice, 1991, by Rozanne Hawksley. The artist drew inspiration from memories of her grandmother, who was widowed in the First World War.

WELCOME TO THE IMPERIAL WAR MUSEUM

P9-DNN-591

This national Museum devoted to the twentieth century is a place of great diversity. Its exhibits range from tanks and aircraft to personal letters and ration books; they include films and sound recordings, and some of the century's best-known paintings.

Our subject is conflicts involving Britain or the Commonwealth since 1914. That gives the Museum enormous scope - we exist to record and explain the two world wars and many other conflicts fought since 1945, to examine what led up to them as well as what happened during and after them.

This is not a Museum of the distant past, but about people still alive today, their parents and grandparents. The wars of the twentieth century have affected each and every one of us in some way, and the Museum is here to tell all our stories. So we are free to cover all human life - heroes and villains and the millions who are neither - and all human experience, on the battlefield and at home, whether of civilian housewives or farm or factory workers or conscientious objectors or the victims of the Holocaust, as much as of generals and soldiers, sailors and airmen.

Not everything is on display. The Museum's collections are far too extensive for that. Its reference departments are a rich source of information for the many people who come to study in them. The archives of documents and printed material, film, photographs, sound recordings, works of art and three dimensional objects are briefly described later in this handbook.

The Museum has other branches, also open to the public: the Second World War cruiser HMS Belfast at her moorings on the River Thames; the Cabinet War Rooms, the secret Government headquarters below Whitehall; and the IWM Duxford, one of the country's most comprehensive air museums, sited on a former Battle of Britain station.

At all the Museum's branches we endeavour to make recent history accessible and interesting. We hope that everyone who comes to see us will find their visit stimulating and entertaining, and we welcome suggestions of how we can improve our displays and our service. Please let us know if you have any comments, whether approving or disapproving.

Robert Crawford

1

2

The Large Exhibits Gallery, the impressive central space of the redevelopment of the original building, is the setting for some of the most important weapons and vehicles in the collections, including guns, tanks and aircraft.

Examples of several of the artillery pieces used in the world wars can be seen. Of special interest is a 13-pounder gun of E Battery, Royal Horse Artillery, which on 22 August 1914 fired the first British shell on land in the First World War. The 18-pounder was the standard British field gun and earned a reputation as one of the most reliable weapons of its type. Nearly 100 million rounds of 18-pounder ammunition were expended in France alone between 1914 and 1918, an average of 43 rounds for every minute of the war. The 75 mm, the French equivalent of the 18-pounder, was the first gun to be fitted with a recoil system and was renowned for its accuracy and rapidity of fire.

Heavy artillery includes a British 9.2-inch howitzer and a 60-pounder gun, which had a range of seven miles.

An unusual observation device is a German mast periscope designed for use behind buildings and in woods.

The tank - a British invention - was developed to break the deadlock of trench warfare. The Mark V represented an important advance in tank design. Introduced in 1918, it carried a crew of eight and could travel at a speed of over 4 miles an hour.

1 *'J' Battery, Royal Horse Artillery, in open positions, 1914. Q60751*

2 *British 9.2-inch howitzer.*

3 *Views of the Large Exhibits Gallery.*

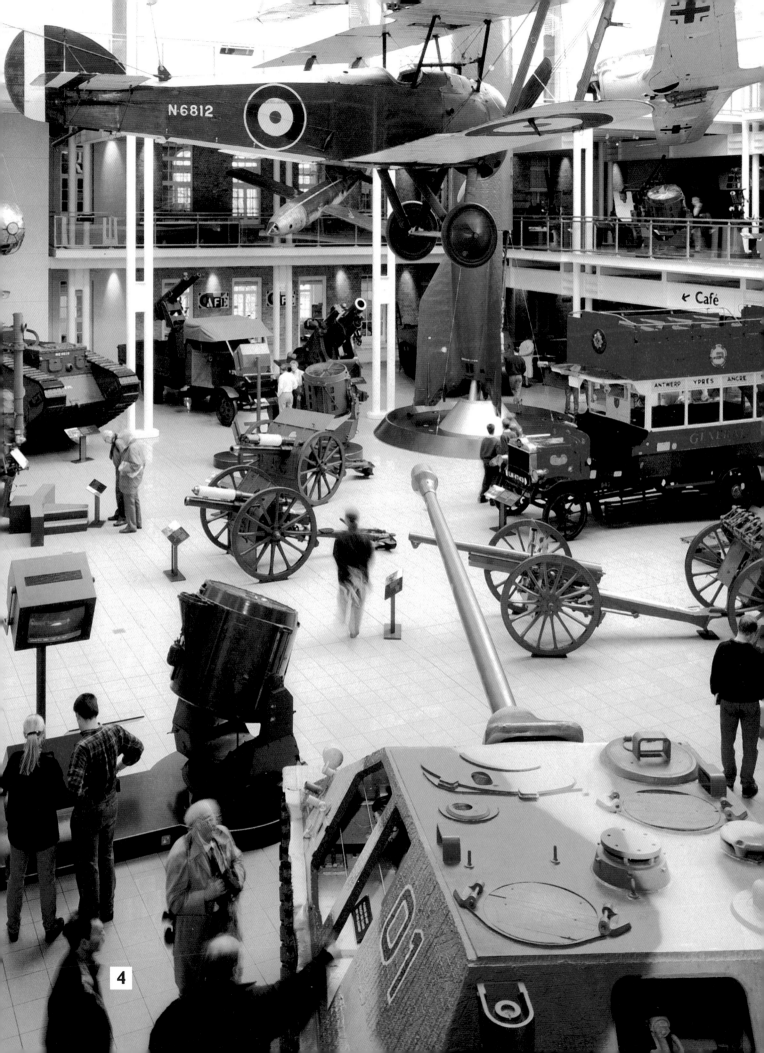

1

The earliest of the five Second World War tanks in the gallery is the British Infantry Mark II 'Matilda', a type which gave a good account of itself in France in 1940 and against the Italians in the Western Desert in the winter of 1940-1941. The German 8.8 cm was the only anti-tank gun able to penetrate its thick armour plating. The arrival of the M3 Grant in the Western Desert in the summer of 1942 at last gave the hard-pressed British Eighth Army a tank which could match the Panzer Mark IIIs and IVs of the German Afrika Korps. The slow but heavily armoured Churchill was one of the more successful British tanks and saw service in Tunisia, Italy and North West Europe. The principal armoured weapon of the Allied armies was the American-built M4 Sherman, which was produced in greater numbers than any other tank. The Russian T-34 combined speed with endurance and was perhaps the outstanding tank of the war, playing a decisive role in the great armoured battles on the Eastern Front.

The two remaining Second World War military vehicles are a Daimler armoured car and the ubiquitous jeep, of which more than 600,000 were built.

Anti-tank weapons include the formidable Jagdpanther, an 8.8 cm self-propelled tank destroyer; and a German 5 cm anti-tank gun.

The 25-pounder was the standard British field gun of the Second World War. The 5.5-inch gun equipped British medium artillery regiments and served in all the major theatres from 1942. The Nebelwerfer projectile launcher was employed by Germans in considerable numbers in the later stages of the war and the terrifying scream of its rockets was a familiar sound to Allied troops in Normandy in 1944. A 4.7-ton shell from a massive German 80 cm gun is displayed. Nicknamed *Schwerer Gustav* ('Heavy Gustav'), it was the largest gun ever built but fired only 48 rounds during the war - against Sebastopol in 1942.

1 *Grant tanks lined up in the Western Desert, 17 February 1942. E8487*

2 *M4 Sherman tank.*

2

The first British shot in the First World War was fired by a 4-inch gun from the destroyer HMS *Lance*. Another naval exhibit of note is the 5.5-inch gun from HMS *Chester* which the sixteen-year-old Boy First Class Jack Cornwell was serving when he was mortally wounded at the Battle of Jutland. He was posthumously awarded the Victoria Cross.

By the First World War the use of submarines and mines presented new threats to shipping. One of the weapons on display is a 10.5 cm gun from the submarine U98. Another German weapon from the First World War is a moored contact mine.

An unusual example of a Second World War submarine is the German one-man Biber, which was hastily developed for operations against the Allied invasion flotilla in 1944. Another specialised underwater craft is the Italian 'human torpedo', which was employed with spectacular success against British battleships in Alexandria harbour in 1941. The *Tamzine* is the smallest surviving fishing boat to have taken part in the evacuation of British and French troops from Dunkirk in 1940.

1 *U35 in the Mediterranean, 1917. Q53010*

2 *German one-man Biber submarine.*

3 *The fishing boat Tamzine.*

1

2

G

3

The military possibilities of aircraft were not fully appreciated in 1914 but by the end of the war they had begun to exert a significant influence on the conduct of land operations. Two First World War aircraft are displayed, an early two-seat reconnaissance machine - the BE2c - and a Sopwith Camel 2F1, the naval version of the celebrated British fighter. Also on view is the observation car from a Zeppelin (probably LZ90), which was found near Colchester after an air raid in 1916.

4

The collection of Second World War aircraft includes a Supermarine Spitfire Mark 1A which saw action in the Battle of Britain. Another exceptional Allied fighter was the North American P-51 Mustang. With auxiliary fuel tanks it could escort bombers of the United States Eighth Air Force to Berlin and back and it made a crucial contribution to the battle for air supremacy over Germany. German Second World War aircraft consist of a Focke Wulf 190 and a Heinkel 162. The radial-engined FW190, which the RAF first encountered in 1941, was one of the fastest and most manoeuvrable fighters of the war. The HE162 'Salamander' jet fighter was rushed into production in 1944 in a vain attempt to combat the Allied air offensive.

5

1 *This BE2A, photographed near Whitby in August 1914, was the first British aircraft to land in France after the outbreak of the First World War. The pilot, Lieutenant H D Harvey-Kelly, is relaxing at the foot of the haystack. Q54985*

2 *Royal Aircraft Factory BE2c.*

3 *Lieutenant-Colonel J D Landers, commander of the 78th Fighter Group at Duxford, with his P-51D Mustang, 'Big Beautiful Doll', on 24 March 1945. The Museum's Mustang has been painted to represent this aircraft. HU31358*

4 *North American P-51 Mustang.*

5 *Battle of Britain Spitfire Mark 1A.*

1

The German *Vergeltungswaffen* (reprisal weapons), the V1 and V2, were launched against England in 1944. The V1, known as the 'doodlebug' or 'buzz bomb' was a jet-propelled pilotless aircraft with a speed of about 400 miles per hour. The V2 rocket travelled faster than sound and was impossible to intercept. A total of over 6,500 V weapons fell on London and the South East, killing 8,938 people.

The casing of this 'Little Boy' atomic bomb is of the type dropped on Hiroshima in 1945.

The post-war Polaris was the first submarine-based ballistic missile and has been Britain's independent nuclear deterrent since 1968.

1 *V1 flying bomb. CL3433*

2 *V2 rocket.*

3 *'Little Boy' atomic bomb casing.*

3

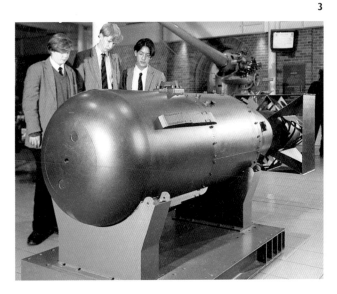

2

1

The exhibits in this area chiefly relate to air warfare. They include a one-pounder anti-aircraft gun, which in September 1915 fired (unsuccessfully) at the first Zeppelin to raid the City of London; the cockpit sections of a Mitsubishi A6M Zero-Sen fighter - the Japanese equivalent of the Spitfire - and of an Avro Lancaster and a Handley Page Halifax, which together formed the backbone of the Royal Air Force's bombing offensive against Germany; a German 8.8 cm high velocity anti-aircraft gun which was also used, with devastating effect, in an anti-tank role; part of the fuselage and one of the Daimler-Benz engines from the Messerschmitt 110 in which Rudolf Hess flew to Scotland in May 1941; and German 'Small Würzburg' radar equipment.

Post-Second World War exhibits include a BAC Thunderbird 2, a surface-to-air guided missile designed to intercept fast high-flying aircraft; and a 20 mm twin-mounted anti-aircraft gun captured from the Argentinians during the Falklands War in 1982.

Also on this floor is the Survival at Sea exhibition which tells the story of the Merchant Navy in the Second World War.

2

3

1 Lancasters of RAF Bomber Command attacking Bremen, 21 March 1945. C5101

2 Fuselage section of a Lancaster bomber.

3 Thunderbird missile.

4 Two merchant seamen who survived for seventy days at sea in the jollyboat of the SS Anglo-Saxon which was torpedoed in 1940.

4

The causes of the First World War were complex and are the subject of continuing historical debate. The rise of Germany after 1871 upset the old balance of power in Europe. Tensions were heightened by conflicting national ambitions, economic competition and colonial rivalries. By 1914 an elaborate system of alliances divided Europe into two armed camps. Any incident involving one country threatened to start a chain reaction dragging them all into war. Such an incident occurred at Sarajevo on 28 June 1914 when the heir to the throne of Austria-Hungary, Archduke Franz Ferdinand, was assassinated. By the end of July the armed forces of Europe were mobilising. Britain declared war on Germany on 4 August 1914, shortly after the Kaiser's armies had crossed the Belgian frontier. Britain was the only major European power without a conscript army. Field Marshal Lord Kitchener, Secretary of State for War, believed that the struggle would be long and costly. He at once set about creating volunteer 'New Armies'. By the end of 1915 nearly two and a half million men had enlisted. In 1916 Parliament passed Military Service Acts, which introduced the conscription of men between 18 and 41.

2

3

BRITONS

"WANTS"
YOU

JOIN YOUR COUNTRY'S ARMY!
GOD SAVE THE KING

Reproduced by permission of LONDON OPINION

1   *The 16th (The Queen's) Lancers during the advance from the Marne to the Aisne, September 1914. Q56309*

2, 4   *One of the principal features of the First World War exhibition is a walk-through re-creation of a front line trench on the Somme in the autumn of 1916. Visitors can experience at first hand what it was like to be a Tommy in the trenches. The re-creation is brought to life with special lighting, sound and smell effects.*

3   *The famous Kitchener poster, designed by Alfred Leete.*

4

The German bid to inflict a swift and decisive defeat on France was checked at the Battle of the Marne in September 1914. By then it had become clear that the range, accuracy and fire power of modern weapons, in particular the defensive capability of the machine gun, were such that soldiers could only survive on the battlefield by taking shelter in trenches. Attempts by each side to outflank the other failed and by December 1914 the opposing lines of trenches extended from the English Channel to the Swiss frontier. For four years the combatants sought ways of ending the stalemate of trench warfare. On a tactical level this resulted in successive attempts to breach the enemy trench lines by the use of massive artillery bombardments, the employment of gas and the development of the tank. Trench warfare created a world of its own - at worst a wilderness of shattered trees, barbed wire entanglements and waterlogged craters. Soldiers on both sides had to contend with difficulties of communication and supply, the misery of wet, cold, mud, rats and lice, and the strain of living under the ever-present threat of death or mutilation. The unprecedented number of casualties and the dreadful wounds caused by high-explosive shells stretched and challenged the medical services.

1 *First World War trench equipment: a British Mills bomb, PH anti-gas helmet, trench club and a German stick grenade.*

2 *Third Ypres, 1917: Australian troops passing along a duckboard track through devastated Chateau Wood. E(1914)1220*

2

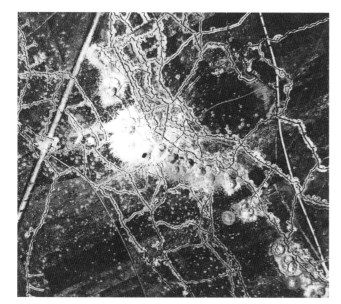

3

As trench warfare settled in on the Western Front, armies became dependent upon the aeroplane as a means of discovering what the enemy was doing. Decisive combats between aircraft were rare in the early months of the war but each side quickly saw the need to win dominance over the opposing air service. This led to the specialisation of aircraft types and hastened the development of the single-seat fighter. From 1916 the air war became a see-saw struggle for supremacy. New aircraft were introduced and tactics constantly refined and improved. By the middle of 1917 air combat had become a matter of team fighting rather than individual scouting. The best-known fighter formation was the 'Richthofen Circus', led by Baron Manfred von Richthofen, an astute tactician and deadly shot, whose distinctive red Albatros became the symbol of dominance over the Western Front. Other 'aces' included the British airmen Captain Albert Ball, Major 'Mick' Mannock and Major James McCudden, Lieutenant Colonel WA 'Billy' Bishop - a Canadian - and the French pilot Capitaine Georges Guynemer.

1 *Second-Lieutenant Albert Ball, a photograph probably taken in 1915. Q69593*

2 *The Last Flight of Captain Ball VC, DSO, MC, 7 May 1917 by Norman G Arnold.*

3 *Aerial photograph taken on 15 July 1915 during preparations for the Battle of Loos. Q60546*

4 *Model of a Fokker DrI triplane.*

1

The most important theatre of the war after France was the Eastern Front, where Germany and Austria-Hungary confronted Russia and Serbia. Much was expected of the Russian 'steamroller'. But by 1917 the Russian army had suffered enormous losses and, despite winning a notable victory against the Austrians in the summer of 1916, was exhausted and demoralised. The October Revolution ended the Russian war effort and on 3 March 1918 Russia and Germany signed a peace treaty at Brest Litovsk. In addition to the Eastern Front there were a number of 'side shows'. Well over a million British, Indian and Dominion troops took part in campaigns against Germany's ally, Turkey - on the Gallipoli peninsula, and in Egypt, Palestine and Mesopotamia. In 1915 an Allied expeditionary force, which eventually grew to 600,000 men, was landed at Salonika to oppose the Bulgarians. French and British contingents were sent to support the Italians in November 1917 after an Austro-German army had inflicted a crushing defeat on them at Caporetto. Further afield, British and German forces fought a long-running campaign in East Africa.

2

1 *Australians at Gallipoli making bombs from empty jam tins. Q13281*

2 *T E Lawrence, Akaba, 1917. Q30212*

3 *Short Magazine Lee-Enfield Mark III rifle used by T E Lawrence. Q44270 By permission of Her Majesty The Queen.*

3

Britain looked to the Royal Navy for protection against invasion and to keep the sea lanes open for essential supplies of food and raw materials. There were engagements between British warships and German commerce raiders in the Indian Ocean, the Pacific and the South Atlantic. The long-awaited clash between the British Grand Fleet and the German High Seas Fleet took place at Jutland on 31 May 1916. Although the battle was tactically indecisive the High Seas Fleet, apart from one or two abortive sorties, remained locked in its bases for the rest of the war. The British blockade of German ports caused great hardship in Germany. The Germans retaliated by mounting a submarine campaign against Allied merchant shipping. This brought Britain close to defeat but also precipitated America's entry into the war in April 1917. The adoption of the convoy system and a substantial increase in British and American shipbuilding enabled the Allies to overcome the U-boat menace.

1 *Sir John Jellicoe on board HMS* Iron Duke. *Q55499*

2 *Ships of the Grand Fleet in line ahead, First World War. Q63698*

3 *German U-boat poster (The U-boats are out) by H R Erdt.*

1

The First World War had an unprecedented effect on civilian life. Shortly after the outbreak of war the government brought in the Defence of the Realm Act, which gave it sweeping powers. News was censored, the coal mines nationalised, land and property requisitioned for military purposes, the sale of alcohol restricted and Summer Time introduced. Food rationing was instituted in 1918. Recruiting caused labour shortages which resulted in large numbers of women doing jobs in industry, transport, agriculture and commerce previously done by men. Some 100,000 women joined the newly formed auxiliary services of the three armed forces. Zeppelin and aircraft raids caused much dislocation and put civilians in the front line for the first time. The war also made its impact on an emotional level, with almost every family being affected by the death or wounding of a relative or friend.

2

1 German incendiary bomb dropped by Zeppelin LZ38 on 31 May 1915 during the first airship raid on London.

2 Ministry of Munitions recruitment poster, 1918.

3 Chilwell Shell-Filling Factory, July 1917. Q30011

3

2

The horror of the Western Front inspired some memorable poetry. The major war poets - Edmund Blunden, Siegfried Sassoon, Robert Graves, Isaac Rosenberg and Wilfred Owen - all had first-hand experience of the trenches. Their poems, written in direct and sometimes brutal language, were a protest against what they saw as the tragic waste and futility of the conflict. The war also provided powerful subject matter for artists such as John and Paul Nash, C R W Nevinson, Stanley Spencer, William Roberts and Eric Kennington. From 1916 they and many others were employed as official war artists to record scenes on the home and fighting fronts.

What passing-bells for these who die as cattle?
- Only the monstrous anger of the guns.
Only the stuttering rifles' rapid rattle
Can patter out their hasty orisons.
No mockeries now for them; no prayers nor bells;
Nor any voice of mourning save the choirs, -
The shrill, demented choirs of wailing shells;
And bugles calling for them from sad shires.

What candles may be held to speed them all?
Not in the hands of boys, but in their eyes
Shall shine the holy glimmers of goodbyes.
The pallor of girls' brows shall be their pall;
Their flowers the tenderness of patient minds,
And each slow dusk a drawing-down of blinds.

Anthem for Doomed Youth by Wilfred Owen

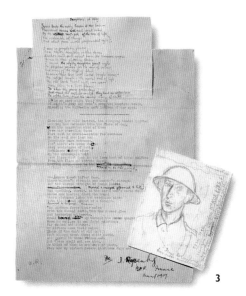

3

1 *Siegfried Sassoon. Copyright Radio Times Hulton Picture Library.*

2 *Sketch for* Over the Top *by John Nash.*

3 *Manuscript by the war poet and artist Isaac Rosenberg.*

Hostilities on the Western Front ceased at 11am on 11 November 1918 when an armistice between Germany and the Allies came into effect. A final settlement, determined by a peace conference, was embodied in the Treaty of Versailles, which was signed by the Germans, under protest, on 28 June 1919. Germany lost territory and its armed forces were greatly reduced. It had to pay massive compensation for war damage and admit its guilt for causing the war. These terms provoked great bitterness in Germany and sowed the seeds of future discord in Europe.

1   Next of Kin memorial plaque.

2   Letters written by Emily Chitticks to her sweetheart Will Martin, who was killed on 27 March 1917. They were returned to her unopened, marked 'Killed in Action'.

3   Pilckem Ridge, Ypres Salient, 22 August 1917. Q2756

Hopes for a lasting peace after the First World War were short-lived. The next two decades witnessed a series of wars and diplomatic crises that pointed the way to a new global conflict. Totalitarian states were established in Italy after 1922 under Benito Mussolini's Fascist party and in Nazi Germany, where Adolf Hitler became Chancellor in 1933. Germany began to rearm and to create an air force. In March 1936 Hitler reoccupied the demilitarised Rhineland and two years later marched into Austria. Shortly afterwards, at the Munich Conference, he persuaded the Western powers to force Czechoslovakia to cede the Sudetenland. In March 1939 Germany occupied the rest of Czechoslovakia. The German invasion of Poland on 1 September 1939 marked the end of the policy of appeasement pursued by the British prime minister, Neville Chamberlain. Britain and France declared war on Germany on 3 September, though they were unable to intervene effectively on Poland's behalf.

1 Adolf Hitler addressing the Nazi party rally at Nuremberg, 1936. FLM1531

2 Neville Chamberlain waving the text of his agreement with Hitler on his return from Munich, 30 September 1938. D2239

3 Nazi election poster.

4 Models of Nazi standard bearers, made in Germany by Elastolin in the 1930s.

Having failed to prevent the defeat of Poland, which was overwhelmed in a campaign lasting under three weeks, Britain and France were faced with the prospect of a long and costly war with Germany. Britain braced itself for an all-out German attack and civil defence plans were put into effect. Although there was some action at sea, there was little activity on land or in the air. The war developed a sense of unreality which earned it the title of the 'Phoney War'.

In the spring of 1940 Germany launched Blitzkrieg (lightning war) attacks in Scandinavia and Western Europe. German forces invaded Norway in April and the Low Countries and France on 10 May - the day on which Winston Churchill became prime minister. The main German attack was directed not against the heavily fortified Maginot Line but through the lightly defended Ardennes. German tanks and assault troops with close air support broke through the French line and drove northwards towards the sea, splitting the Allied armies in two. The British Expeditionary Force and the French First Army were cornered at Dunkirk but 338,000 managed to escape, thanks to a hasty but effective evacuation operation mounted across the English Channel. The German advance against the bulk of the French forces continued until an armistice was agreed on 22 June.

1 Blackout poster.

2 A child's 'Mickey Mouse' gas mask.

3 Evacuation card game.

4 British troops wading out to a rescue ship off Dunkirk, 1940. HU41240

After the collapse of France, Britain stood alone. In July 1940 Hitler directed that plans be drawn up for an invasion of the British mainland, codenamed Operation 'Sealion'. But before the invasion could be mounted the Germans had to win command of the skies over southern England by defeating the Royal Air Force. The Luftwaffe began its main offensive on 13 August 1940, attacking airfields, radar stations, ports and aircraft factories. Fighter Command was down to its last reserves when, on 7 September, the assault was unexpectedly switched to London. The Luftwaffe's efforts intensified but so did its losses. On 17 September Hitler postponed 'Sealion' indefinitely.

2

3

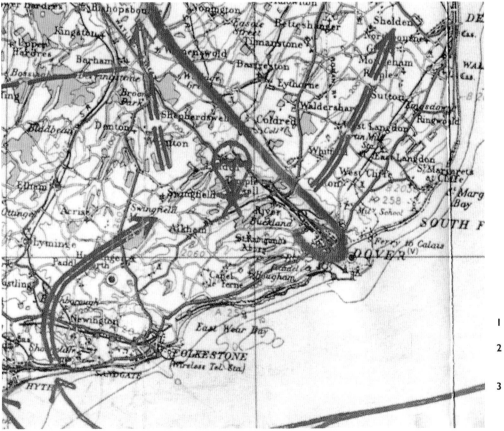

1 Battle of Britain poster. (detail)

2 Wreckage of Dornier aircraft under guard, 18 August 1940. HU3122

3 Detail from a German invasion map for Operation 'Sealion', 1940.

1

Unable to launch an invasion, Germany tried instead to bomb Britain into submission. The Blitz, the period of most sustained bombing, lasted from September 1940 until the late spring of 1941. London was attacked on fifty-seven consecutive nights and fifteen other British cities, notably Coventry, suffered extensive damage. Over 41,000 British civilians were killed and 137,000 injured. Britain came under heavy attack again in 1944 from Germany's secret weapons, the VI and the V2. The country endured not only air raids but also severe shortages of food and raw materials. Life in Britain was hard and drab. Every kind of resource was mobilised for the war effort. The conscription of men and women into civil as well as military occupations was introduced: by the middle of 1944 over 460,000 women were in the services and six and a half million were engaged in civilian war work. Britain became home to thousands of refugees as well as foreign servicemen, especially Americans, once preparations began for an Allied invasion of Europe.

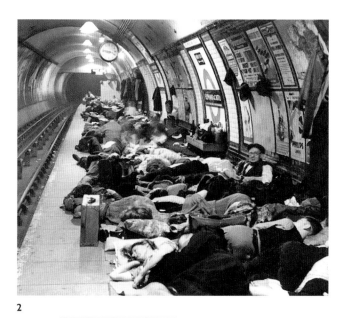

2

3

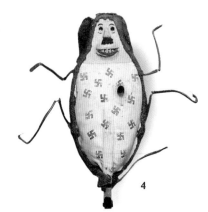

4

1 Coupons Required, 1941 *by Leonora Green.*

2 *The Elephant and Castle underground station, 11 November 1940. D1568*

3 *Home Front posters.*

4 *'Squander bug' rifle target. The 'Squander Bug' was a popular cartoon character used to persuade people to avoid waste.*

5 *The Blitz Experience: a carefully researched reconstruction of an air-raid shelter and a blitzed street in 1940. Appropriate sights, sounds and smells evoke for visitors a sensation of being caught in the bombing of London during the Second World War.*

1

For Britain, dependent upon imports, command of the sea was vital. The German surface fleet, which included the battleships *Bismarck* and *Tirpitz* as well as other powerful modern warships, represented a constant menace to Allied merchant shipping; in the event it did relatively little damage. The flow of raw materials, food, munitions and men from North America was the key to Britain's survival. As in the First World War, German submarines posed the biggest threat to the supply routes. The U-boats inflicted losses averaging 96 ships a month in 1942 but by the middle of 1943 the Battle of the Atlantic had swung in favour of the Allies. Better anti-submarine weapons and detection devices, trained convoy support groups, escort carriers and long-range aircraft all helped to defeat the U-boats. Shipping in the Mediterranean and convoys carrying Allied supplies to Russia were also at risk. Out of 40 Arctic convoys, 89 merchant ships and 18 warships were sunk.

2

3

THE
BRITISH NAVY
guards the freedom of us all

4

1 *HMS Scylla during the passage of convoy JW53 to Russia in February 1943. A15365*

2 *The carriers Indomitable and Eagle during Operation 'Pedestal', August 1942. A15961h*

3 *The British Navy. Poster by Frank Mason.*

4 *Model of a German Type VII U-boat.*

I

2

1 *General Montgomery in his Grant tank. This tank is displayed in the Large Exhibits Gallery. E18980(KT)*

2 *Ukulele made at Tobruk in 1941.*

3 *British Second World War propaganda poster.*

As Germany completed the domination of Western Europe, fighting began in the Mediterranean theatre. German forces swept through Greece in the spring of 1941 and in an airborne invasion of Crete forced British troops to evacuate the island. Earlier, an Italian attack on Egypt had been successfully repulsed but the German Afrika Korps, sent to reinforce the Italians early in 1941, posed a new threat in the Western Desert under the aggressive leadership of General Rommel. In June 1942 Rommel captured the important port of Tobruk. Two months later Lieutenant-General Montgomery took command of the British Eighth Army and ended its series of defeats by winning a decisive victory at the Battle of El Alamein in November. Operation 'Torch', the landing of three British and American armies under the command of General Eisenhower, led in May 1943 to the surrender of the Axis forces in North Africa. The capture of Sicily in August 1943 and the subsequent invasion of Italy gave the Allies their first foothold on the European mainland since 1940. German forces seized control of Italy when the Italians agreed to an armistice with the Allies. The advance through Italy was slow and costly but by the spring of 1945 the Allies had reached the north Italian plains. The Germans surrendered unconditionally on 2 May.

3

Britain develops new desert tactics. Tough, well-trained infantry clear the way for tanks in North Africa

THE DOWNFALL OF THE DICTATORS IS ASSURED

1

Strategic, economic and ideological motives lay behind Hitler's decision to order the invasion of Russia. The German offensive, Operation 'Barbarossa', began on 22 June 1941, taking the Soviet forces by surprise. Employing well-tried Blitzkrieg tactics, the three-million strong force struck deep into the Soviet heartland, capturing whole Russian armies before coming to a halt on the outskirts of Leningrad and Moscow. In December 1941 the Soviet Union surprised the Germans by mounting a counter-offensive, easing the pressure on Moscow. Hitler turned his attention to the south and attacked in the Caucasus in the spring of 1942. His armies were comprehensively defeated at Stalingrad early in 1943 and in the Battle of Kursk in the summer, which cost the Wehrmacht half a million men. The Germans, fighting doggedly, were steadily driven from Soviet territory.

2

ПОДВИГАМЪ ДОБЛЕСТИ СЛАВА, ЧЕСТЬ, ПАМЯТЬ.

ПУСТЬ ВДОХНОВЛЯЕТ ВАС В ЭТОЙ ВОЙНЕ МУЖЕСТВЕННЫЙ ОБРАЗ НАШИХ ВЕЛИКИХ ПРЕДКОВ!
И. СТАЛИН

3

4

1 *Russian infantry advancing during the Soviet winter offensive of 1942. RUS2109*

2 *German Panzer Mark III and assault troops, a photograph probably taken in the Ukraine in 1941. COL158*

3 *Russian patriotic poster.*

4 *German straw 'snow' boots used on the Eastern Front.*

1

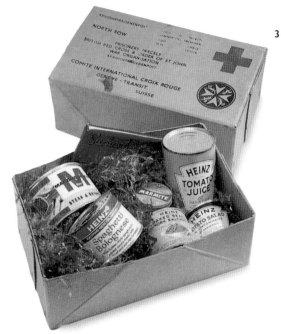

2

In the wake of German victory came Nazi exploitation of the conquered territories. Occupied Europe's agricultural and industrial output was channelled to meet Germany's needs, regardless of the deprivation this caused to home markets. The Nazis imposed repressive racial and political policies. Although the severity of German rule varied greatly from country to country, no community remained untouched. The first attempts at resistance in Occupied Europe were largely isolated and ill-coordinated acts of personal opposition. But with the passage of time, men, women and children joined together to confront their oppressors. An alternative to Nazi propaganda was provided by the illegal press. Escape lines and intelligence networks helped the Allied war effort. Where circumstances permitted, resisters carried out a guerilla war against the German and collaborationist forces. However, effective armed resistance was largely dependent on support from one of the Allies' own clandestine organisations.

1, 4 *Colditz Castle and improvised tools made by POWs at Colditz to build a glider as a means of escape.*

2 *Members of the Dutch underground movement. BU2887*

3 *An example of a Red Cross parcel sent to British prisoners of war in Germany during the Second World War.*

3

4

1

The strategic air offensive played a major, but not decisive, role in the defeat of Germany by attacking the enemy's economic strength and will to resist. The ineffectiveness of operations up to the end of 1941 exposed the weakness of the RAF. Aircraft, bombs and navigational equipment were inadequate and losses in daylight raids caused Bomber Command to switch to night attacks. From February 1942 Air Marshal Harris adopted the 'area' bombing of German cities in an attempt to disrupt industrial production and morale. On 31 May 1942 the first 'thousand bomber' raid was launched against Cologne. In August 1942 the American Eighth Air Force joined the offensive and began precision daylight bombing against key targets. In 1943 and 1944 the RAF attacked the Ruhr, Hamburg and Berlin. Enemy fighters took a heavy toll and German war production actually increased until July 1944. The arrival of long-range escort fighters transformed the bomber offensive in the last phase of the war. A Bomber Command attack in support of Allied land operations culminated in the destruction of the historic city of Dresden in February 1945, causing thousands of civilian deaths. The bomber offensive was extremely costly, with Bomber Command losing 55,573 aircrew and 1,570 ground staff.

1 Wing-Commander Guy Gibson, VC. MH6673

2 Dresden, photographed a few years after the war. HU3321

3 American B-17 Flying Fortresses. HU4052

4 USAAF leather flying jacket.

5 'Take off': Interior of a Bomber Aircraft by Dame Laura Knight.

3

4

1

In 1944 the Eastern Front turned increasingly in Russia's favour and in June the Allied invasion of Normandy opened the campaign for the liberation of Western Europe. On 6 June 1944 ('D-Day'), Operation 'Overlord' began, under the American Supreme Commander, General Eisenhower. The assault forces, under the command of General Montgomery, came ashore from some 4,000 landing craft escorted by 600 warships, with air support from more than 10,000 Allied aircraft. Over 156,000 British, Canadian and American troops were landed on the first day, making this the largest combined operation in history. After a month of

2

I *Commando troops going ashore on D-Day, 6 June 1944. B5103*

2 *Sleeve badges worn by members of the American 101st 'Screaming Eagles' Airborne Division (left) and the First Polish Armoured Division (right).*

3 *Rocket-firing Typhoons at the Falaise Gap, Normandy 1944 by Frank Wootton.*

3

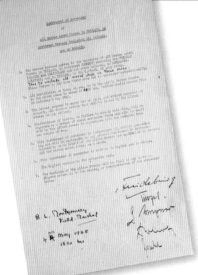

heavy fighting Caen fell to the British and Canadians. At the end of July American forces broke through the German defences and advanced rapidly south and east. Paris was liberated on 25 August, Brussels on 3 September. Montgomery's bold plan to open a 'back door' into Germany through Holland ended in failure on 26 September when the British 1st Airborne Division was forced to withdraw after seizing a vital river bridge at Arnhem. A daring German counter-attack in the Ardennes in December was repulsed and in March 1945 Allied troops crossed the Rhine. As agreed at the Yalta Conference in February 1945, the Western Allies halted on the Elbe, allowing the Russians to take Berlin. In the last months of the war, Hitler's mental and physical health deteriorated rapidly and on 30 April he committed suicide in his underground bunker. On 4 May German forces in North-West Europe surrendered to the Commander-in-Chief of the 21st Army Group, Field Marshal Montgomery. The instrument of Germany's unconditional surrender was signed at Eisenhower's headquarters in Rheims on 7 May. Victory in Europe (VE) Day was celebrated the following day.

1 Paratroops of the 1st Airborne Division firing on German positions with a 3-inch mortar, Arnhem, 20 September 1944. BU1098

2 The signing of the Instrument of Surrender at 21st Army Group Headquarters, Lüneburg Heath, 4 May 1945. BU5207

3 The surrender document. U52168

4 Battledress blouse which belonged to Field Marshal Montgomery.

By 1941 Japanese ambitions in Asia and the Pacific had led
to a serious deterioration in relations with the United States.
On 7 December 1941, without a declaration of war,
Japanese carrier-borne aircraft attacked the US Pacific Fleet
at its base at Pearl Harbor in the Hawaiian Islands and put
most of it out of action. Congress declared war on Japan
the next day. The Allies were ill-prepared to defend their
possessions in the Far East and by the summer of 1942 the
Japanese had overrun the Philippines, Malaya, Burma and the
Dutch East Indies. Japan's early successes resulted in the
capture of hundreds of thousands of Allied military and
civilian personnel, who had to endure malnutrition, disease,
forced labour and appalling living conditions. Over a quarter
of them died. At Midway in 1942, which like other naval
battles in the Pacific was dominated by the aircraft carrier,
the Japanese suffered their first major defeat of the war.

2

1 *British mortar team in action,
Imphal-Kohima, July 1944. INDA4723*

2 British Women and Children interned
in a Japanese Prison Camp, Syme
Road, Singapore *by Leslie Cole, 1945.*

3 Prisoner 111 with Dysentry, Changi
Gaol *by Ronald Searle, 1944.*

3

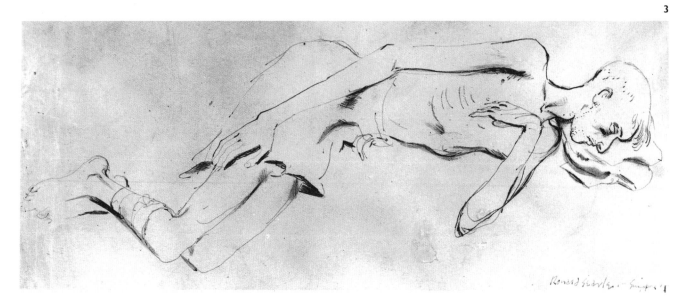

Soon they were being pushed back throughout their Pacific empire. General MacArthur's forces fought their way through New Guinea to the Philippines; in another series of operations the Solomon Islands were recaptured after savage resistance by the Japanese. In the central Pacific, Admiral Nimitz carried out a series of amphibious operations which brought the Americans within bombing range of Tokyo. In the Battle of Imphal-Kohima in 1944 the British Fourteenth Army under General Slim won a decisive victory which removed the Japanese threat to India. By the spring of 1945 the Americans were preparing to invade Japan. President Truman decided to use the newly developed atomic bomb to end the war. Two bombs were dropped - on Hiroshima on 6 August 1945 and on Nagasaki three days later. On 14 August the Japanese surrendered unconditionally.

1

1 *The atomic explosion at Nagasaki, 9 August 1945. MH2629*

2 *Relics from Hiroshima and Nagasaki.*

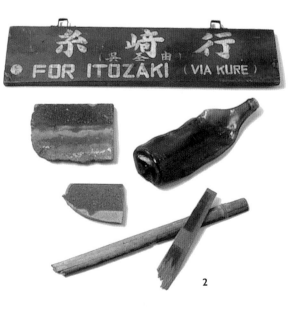

2

The end of the Second World War did not bring an end to conflict. There has been fighting somewhere in the world almost every day since 1945.

Post-war divisions between east and western Europe led to a prolonged Cold War. The development of the atomic bomb precipitated a nuclear arms race, with both sides possessing the means to destroy the world. The collapse of communism in Europe, marked by the pulling down of the Berlin Wall in 1989 and the break-up of the Soviet Union, ended the Cold War and diminished the threat of nuclear war in the west.

Elsewhere in the world, the ending of colonial rule and attempts to prevent the spread of communism led to fighting in many countries. During the Cold War period the US and the Soviet Union tried to exert their influence in other parts of the world and sometimes prolonged or complicated existing conflicts.

In Asia, China, North Korea and North Vietnam came under communist control and communists in Malaya made a bid for power. Some of the largest and longest post-war conflicts followed. America led the fight against communism, but British and Commonwealth forces fought in Korea, Malaya and Indonesia, and Australian and New Zealand forces fought alongside the Americans and South Vietnamese in the Vietnam War.

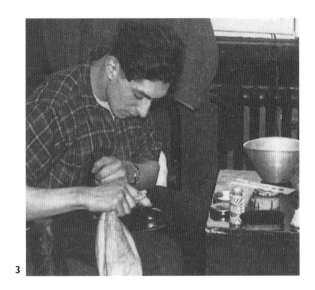

2

3

1 Military Cross awarded to Second Lieutenant H A J Stacpoole who commanded the Assault Pioneer Platoon, 1st Battalion, The Duke of Wellington's Regiment (West Riding), at the Battle of the Hook, Korea, in May 1953. The service medals are for Suez, Korea and Cyprus.

2 National Service recruit arriving at Pirbright Depot.

3 A National Serviceman bulling his kit for inspection, 1954. Photo courtesy D Peterman. HU5149

In Africa the granting of independence to former colonies was often accompanied or followed by fighting and civil war. Famine and disease among the many refugees was a major cause of loss of life.

Disagreements over territory and access to oil fields have led to conflict in the Middle East. Britain's political influence in this region declined after the Suez Crisis of 1956. Iraq's seizure of Kuwait in 1990 was countered by the formation of a multi-national Coalition force. During the Gulf Conflict Britain made a major contribution, with the largest deployment of its forces on active service since the Second World War. The Coalition protected Saudi Arabia, also under threat of an Iraqi invasion, and in 1991 ejected the Iraqis from Kuwait.

Britain's armed forces have undergone major changes since 1945. National Service ended in 1963, after a reduction in Britain's colonial commitments and the development of an independent nuclear deterrent. Britain's membership of NATO, together with advances in technology, have resulted in a smaller but better equipped force able to deal with a wide variety of tasks. Unexpected crises such as the Argentine invasion of the Falklands in 1982 required a rapid military response from Britain. Longer-term deployments of British forces have included support for the Royal Ulster Constabulary during the 'troubles' in Northern Ireland and, increasingly, a peacekeeping role with the United Nations in places such as Bosnia-Herzegovina and Kosovo.

2

3

I *Campaign for Nuclear Disarmament symbol.*

2 *A Sea Harrier taking off from HMS* Hermes *for Combat Air Patrol in May 1982, during the Falklands War. Photograph by Lt Cdr R Nichol. RKD2343*

3 *Major J Potter of B Company, 1st Battalion, The Royal Scots, with Iraqi prisoners, during the Gulf War land offensive, 1991. Photograph by Mike Moore, Today newspaper. GLF587*

Ein Volk, ein Reich, ein Führer! 1

The Holocaust Exhibition traces the Nazi persecution and murder of Europe's Jews from 1933 to 1945. It also covers other groups targeted by the Nazis, such as Gypsies (Roma and Sinti), Poles, Soviet prisoners of war, the disabled, Jehovah's Witnesses and homosexuals. Arranged over two floors, the Exhibition uses original artefacts, documents and film, much of which has never been seen in this country. Specially recorded testimony from sixteen Holocaust survivors provides a poignant personal angle.

This exhibition is not recommended for children under 14. Parents or carers wishing to take younger children into the Exhibition may do so at their own discretion.
Children must be closely supervised at all times.

The Exhibition is situated on two floors.
Upper Floor The November 1918 Armistice brought peace, but Europe was left scarred and in economic depression. In Germany there was resentment of what was seen as a punishing peace treaty, and many blamed the Jews for the country's defeat.

1920-1933 saw the steady rise of the new National Socialist German Workers Party - the Nazi Party - led by Adolf Hitler. In 1933 Hitler became Chancellor of Germany, and a reign of terror began, with political opponents sent to concentration camps. The first major anti-Jewish measure, a boycott of Jewish businesses, took place on 1 April 1933.

Central to Nazi ideology was antisemitism, a centuries-old prejudice which was prevalent throughout Europe. The Nazis saw themselves as a 'Master Race' and wanted to cleanse Germany - and Europe - of 'alien' influences, including Jews and Gypsies. From 1933 anyone alleged to be disabled

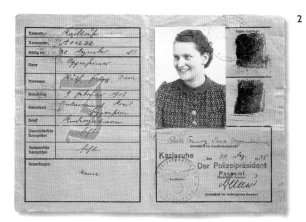

1 One People, One Reich, One Führer: *a 1938 Nazi poster.*

2 *Identity card of a Jewish woman stamped with a 'J' under a 1938 Nazi regulation.*

3 *Arrival of a* Kindertransport *at Harwich, December 1938. Courtesy Institute of Contemporary History and Wiener Library, London.*

3

or mentally 'unfit' was sterilised - a measure intended to prevent the contamination of the 'Aryan' race.

The Nazis used propaganda to spread hatred of Jews and passed antisemitic legislation which stripped Jews of citizenship and progressively barred them from professions. Only during the Berlin 1936 Olympic Games was this public hostility to the Jews relaxed for foreign visitors.

From March 1936 Hitler set about reclaiming the lands lost after the First World War and expanding Germany's borders. German troops entered the Rhineland, Austria, the Sudetenland, then the rest of Czechoslovakia and Memel in Lithuania. Jews in these territories began to suffer and many sought refuge abroad.

On 9 November 1938 Nazi stormtroopers rampaged through Germany's streets, attacking Jewish businesses and killing ninety-one Jews - an event known as *Kristallnacht* (the Night of Broken Glass). With violence now an ever-present threat, many more Jews sought desperately to emigrate, but most countries would admit only limited numbers in a time of economic hardship. Some 50,000 came to Britain, 10,000 under the *Kindertransport* scheme which brought unaccompanied children to this country.

War broke out on 1 September 1939 when Hitler invaded Poland. In October Hitler ordered the killing of thousands of mentally ill and disabled people. They were murdered by gas or lethal injection in the first Nazi mass murder programme.

Lower Floor Germany swiftly conquered much of Poland, with the Soviet Army securing Eastern Poland. In the reign of terror that followed, thousands of Poles were murdered

I *A Jewish family in Berlin wearing yellow stars prescribed under the 1941 Nazi regulation. Courtesy Süddeutscher Verlag Bilderdienst, Germany.*

2 *Jewish stores in Berlin wrecked on* Kristallnacht. *Courtesy BPK Berlin, Germany.*

3 *Jews from Bedzin, Poland. Only five people in this photograph survived the Holocaust. Courtesy Mrs Helen Stone*

4 *Yellow star of a Dutch Jew.*

and Jews were especially singled out. They were stripped of property, made to do forced labour and concentrated in ghettos. Details of Nazi crimes reached Britain, usually through couriers working for the Polish Government-in-Exile based in London. Then, in June 1941, Germany invaded the Soviet Union. SS murder squads - *Einsatzgruppen* - shot entire Jewish communities, often assisted by local volunteers. In two days nearly 40,000 Jews were shot at Babi Yar, on the outskirts of Kiev. In the ghettos of occupied Poland, Jews either worked for rations or smuggled food in a desperate attempt to stay alive. Conditions worsened, however, and 500,000 Jews eventually died from disease or hunger. In March 1942 the Nazis began to move people out of the ghettos for 'Resettlement in the East': deportation to death camps.

In an attempt to improve on shooting as a killing method, the Nazis started to murder Jews with gas, firstly in vans, and then in chambers at four death camps - Chelmno, Belzec, Sobibor and Treblinka. Rumours of the camps reached the ghettos. In Warsaw, the Jews revolted against the Nazis. Starving and with few weapons, they held out for a month before being killed or captured. Prisoners at Sobibor and Treblinka also staged revolts.

From September 1941, Jews in Nazi-occupied countries were forced to wear a yellow star. This preceded large scale deportation to camps in packed railcars, often without food or water. Some Jews were hidden by non-Jewish friends or family; others were betrayed. Timetables were co-ordinated to transport Jews speedily to their deaths.

The last, and largest, death camp to go into operation was Auschwitz II-Birkenau. A million Jews, thousands of Gypsies

1 Jews being deported by railcar to a death camp.
Courtesy BPK, Berlin, Germany.

2 Items brought to Auschwitz by Jewish deportees.
Courtesy Panstwowe Muzeum Auschwitz-Birkenau w Oswiecimiu, Poland.

3 Arrival of Hungarian Jews in Auschwitz II-Birkenau.
Courtesy Yad Vashem Archives, Israel.

and other victims were murdered in its gas chambers. As the trains arrived, Jewish victims were selected by an SS doctor. About one in five was sent for slave labour, the rest gassed immediately. Auschwitz was one of an immense system of camps in Nazi-occupied territory, in which Jews not killed on arrival joined other prisoner groups deemed enemies of the Reich. Life expectancy was short.

The news of the extermination of Jews led to calls for action. The general response of the Allied governments was that the way to save lives was to win the war.

As the Nazis retreated before the Soviet advance, they tried to hide evidence of their crimes, destroying camps and digging up and burning the remains of thousands of their victims. Prisoners were force-marched to camps inside the Reich. Thousands died on these 'death marches'.

Majdanek, captured by the Soviet Army in July 1944, was the first concentration camp to be liberated. The Allies did not reach most camps until April 1945, among them Bergen-Belsen, where British troops found the largest single grouping of Jewish survivors. The reports sent from these camps horrified the world. Although trials of war criminals were held, many perpetrators escaped justice.

The Holocaust Exhibition concludes with the words of the survivors whose stories have been heard at intervals throughout the display. They tell us what effect their experiences have had on their lives and of their hope that mankind will learn from this most terrible event of modern times.

1 *Auschwitz registration photograph of a Jewish prisoner.*
   Courtesy Panstwowe Muzeum Auschwitz-Birkenau w Oswiecimiu, Poland.

2 *Shoes taken from prisoners at Majdanek concentration camp.*
   Courtesy Panstwowe Muzeum na Majdanku, Lublin, Poland.

3 *Toy bear belonging to Paul Sondhoff, a Jewish boy hidden for four years in a cupboard by his piano teacher in Vienna.*
   Courtesy the Foster family.

I

The Secret War exhibition reveals for the first time the clandestine world of espionage, covert operations, and the work of Britain's special forces.

It shows how Britain's secret government agencies, MI5 and MI6, have developed since their establishment before the First World War, and how specialist communications technology has been used to gather intelligence and break top-secret codes. The work of the Special Operations Executive is covered through exhibits and film footage which provide an insight into the training of SOE agents to enable them to operate in enemy-held territory in the Second World War. Among the exhibits are bottles of invisible ink used by German spies in the First World War, an original German Enigma cipher machine, codebooks, SOE sabotage devices, and a secret radio used by MI6 agents during the Cold War. Files on individual agents and operations can be accessed through interactive videos.

The exhibition also looks at the history of highly trained elite special forces such as the Special Air Service and the Long Range Desert Group. It includes firearms and equipment used in the Second World War and in more recent conflicts such as the Falklands and the Gulf. There are two dramatic audio-visual presentations: *The Benina Raid*, a daring SAS and LRDG attack on a German airfield in North Africa in 1942; and a reconstruction of *Operation 'Nimrod'*, the SAS operation to release hostages held in the Iranian Embassy in London in 1980.

I *A British army intelligence officer examining captured documents, 1918. Q26945*

2 *Long Range Desert Group Chevrolet 30-cwt truck.*

3 *Enigma enciphering machine.*

2

3

VICTORIA CROSS AND GEORGE CROSS

1

2   **3**

The Victoria Cross and George Cross room houses the Museum's collections of these supreme awards for military and civil gallantry. The centrepiece of the display is the 13-pounder 'Néry' gun and the three VCs won by its crew during the Battle of Mons. The stories of Boy First Class Jack Cornwell, Lieutenant J D Smyth (later Brigadier the Rt Hon Sir John Smyth), Corporal Charles Garforth, Group Captain Leonard Cheshire and other First and Second World War VCs are told. Among the George Crosses are those won by the resistance hero Wing Commander F F E Yeo-Thomas, the 'White Rabbit', and by Lieutenant Robert Davies, who saved St Paul's by defusing a bomb which fell close to the cathedral during the Blitz. Related exhibits include a telescope used by Lieutenant Augustus Agar VC and a beret belonging to Colonel 'H' Jones VC.

4   **5**

1   *The Victoria Cross (left) and the George Cross (right).*

2   *Group Captain Leonard Cheshire, VC. CH13636*

3   *Odette Sansom, GC.*

4   *Lieutenant Robert Davies, GC.*

5   *Colonel 'H' Jones, VC. Photograph Cassidy and Leigh.*

6   *Boy First Class Jack Cornwell, VC. Q27025A*

6

1

The two suites of galleries on the second floor are used for long-term exhibitions of First and Second World War works of art from the Museum's collection. The displays are changed at regular intervals. Works of art are also lent to exhibitions at other galleries. If coming to the Museum to see a particular painting, it is advisable to telephone the Department of Art beforehand to check that the work is available.

The art collection is rich in modern British painting by most of the leading artists of the twentieth century, including Sir William Orpen, Sir John Lavery, Sir George Clausen, Augustus John, Sir Stanley Spencer, Paul Nash and John Nash, Percy Wyndham Lewis, William Roberts, C R W Nevinson and Eric Kennington. The art of the Second World War (which also includes work by Paul Nash and Kennington) was dominated by Henry Moore, Graham Sutherland, John Piper, Anthony Gross, Thomas Hennell, Edward Ardizzone and Edward Bawden, all of whom are represented in the collection.

In addition there are significant holdings of work by Carel Weight, Mervyn Peake, Evelyn Dunbar and Richard Eurich. Recent acquisitions have included works by Edward Burra, Cecil Collins, John Tunnard and Sir Stanley Spencer.

One of the most famous paintings in the Museum's collection, *Gassed* by John Singer Sargent, is shown in the Sargent Room. The other galleries on this floor are used for a programme of temporary exhibitions based on the Museum's own collection of fine and graphic art, supplemented by loans from public and private collections. Contemporary art which addresses the Museum's terms of reference is also part of the programme. Details of temporary exhibitions are available in the Reception area.

1 We are Making a New World *by Paul Nash.*

2 Gassed *by John Singer Sargent.*

3 Shipbuilding on the Clyde: The Furnaces *by Stanley Spencer.*

2

HISTORY OF THE MUSEUM
AND BETHLEM ROYAL HOSPITAL

In 1917 the Cabinet decided that a National War Museum should be set up to collect and display material relating to the Great War, which was then still being fought. The interest taken by the Dominion governments led to the museum being given the title of Imperial War Museum. It was formally established by Act of Parliament in 1920 and a governing Board of Trustees appointed.

The Museum was opened in the Crystal Palace by King George V on 9 June 1920. From 1924 to 1935 it was housed, under very difficult conditions, in two galleries adjoining the former Imperial Institute, South Kensington.

On 7 July 1936 the Duke of York, shortly to become King George VI, reopened the Museum in its present home. The Museum was closed to the public from September 1940 to November 1946 and vulnerable collections were evacuated to stores outside London. Most of the exhibits survived the war, but a Short seaplane, which had flown at the Battle of Jutland, was shattered when a German bomb fell on the Naval Gallery on 31 January 1941 and some of the naval models were damaged by blast.

At the outset of the Second World War the Museum's terms of reference were enlarged to cover both world wars and they were again extended in 1953 to include all military operations in which Britain or the Commonwealth have been involved since August 1914.

The building which accommodates the Museum was formerly the central portion of Bethlem Royal Hospital or Bedlam. Designed by James Lewis, it was completed in 1815. Sidney Smirke's dome was added in 1846 and contained the chapel. The east and west wings were demolished in the early 1930s to make room for the park which now surrounds the Museum.

Bethlem Royal Hospital dates back to 1247, when Simon Fitz-Mary, a wealthy alderman and a sheriff of London, founded the Priory of St Mary of Bethlehem on the site which is now part of Liverpool Street station. In the fourteenth century the priory began to specialise in the care of the insane. In 1547 Henry VIII granted the hospital to the City of London.

Bethlem was moved to a new building in Moorfields in 1676. Until 1770 there were no restrictions on visitors, and the lunatics, who were often manacled or chained to the walls, were a public attraction.

The hospital was housed in the present building from 1815 to 1930, when it was transferred to Eden Park near Beckenham, Kent.

Patients included Mary Nicholson who tried to assassinate George III in 1786; Jonathan Martin, committed in 1829 after setting fire to York Minster; the painters Richard Dadd and Louis Wain, famous for his cartoons of cats; Antonia White, author of *Frost in May* and *Beyond the Glass;* and the architect A W N Pugin who designed the Houses of Parliament and St George's Roman Catholic Cathedral opposite the Museum.

1 Bethlem Hospital as it was in 1843 before the building of the dome. MH3478

2 Corridor of Bethlem Royal Hospital. BED10

3 Poster advertising the opening of the Museum at the Crystal Palace, 1920.

4 Poster designed by Edward Wadsworth for the Imperial War Museum, South Kensington, circa 1936.

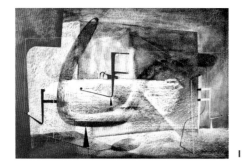

The Imperial War Museum provides extensive access to its 'behind the scenes' collections. No other Museum in the world has a similar breadth of material covering all aspects of twentieth century conflict and beyond. You can arrange to visit or write to the appropriate department or use the IWM web site for further information.

The Department of Art holds one of the leading collections of British twentieth century art. It is rich in fine and graphic art and is especially strong in works commissioned for official purposes during the two world wars. The latter are complemented by the papers of the War Artists' Archive. The sculpture collection includes works by Charles Sargeant Jagger and Jacob Epstein. Altogether there are 14,000 works of fine art. The collection of some 30,000 international war posters is unparalleled in Britain.

The Department of Documents is a major repository for the private papers, amounting to 11,500 collections, of those involved in warfare. It holds the diaries, letters and papers of individuals of all ranks and status, military and civilian. These include manuscript material of the work of war poets and writers such as Isaac Rosenberg and Siegfried Sassoon. Second World War foreign records, a significant source of information on the military and economic history of Germany, Italy and Japan, and the records of the major war crimes trials held by the Allies in Nuremberg and Tokyo are also available.

The Department of Exhibits and Firearms holds an astonishing variety of objects; including artillery, badges, communications equipment, currency, edged weapons, ephemera, flags, firearms, medals and models, toys, transport and uniforms. The displays at all sites offer the best insight into the variety of objects held by the Museum.

1 Anglo Dutch 1942, *tempera on board, by John Tunnard. The painting was purchased with the assistance of the Natonal-Art Collections Fund.*

2 *Personal diary D-Day, 6 June 1944.*

3 *Orders and medals of General Lord Rawlinson of Trent GCB, GCSI, GCVO, KCMG.*

4 *Miss Rosie Newman, amateur camerawoman with 16mm Ciné Kodak Model K camera, circa 1940. HU65393*

5 *British 1st Armoured Division, Gulf War, 1991 (Mike Moore Collection). GLF633*

6 *First World War song sheet.*

6

The Film and Video Archive
is one of the oldest
documentary film archives in
the world; the collection ranges
almost from the birth of
cinema to the present and

4

offers detailed coverage of the military, political and social
history of the twentieth century. The Film and Video Archive
holds 120 million feet of film and 6500 hours of video tape.
Much of the material on the two world wars is 'official' in
origin, derived from British government and military
initiatives to generate material for publicity and record
purposes. There are also contemporary collections, such as
the former library of NATO headquarters in Brussels and
extensive footage received from UNTV Zagreb covering
the conflict in former Yugoslavia. The collection includes a
number of privately shot 'home movies' of life in wartime.

5

The Photograph Archive is one of the largest specialised
archives in the UK and one of the most accessible. It has
over six million photographs. Coverage of the two world
wars reflects the heyday of black and white photography in
the first half of the twentieth century; colour photography
begins to take over in more recent conflicts. The archive is
international in scope although British and Commonwealth

material predominates. American involvement in both world
wars is well covered. The work of professional and private
photographers complements the large official collections.

The Department of Printed Books is a national reference
library on twentieth century conflict involving Britain and
Commonwealth countries. It has some 100,000 books,
25,000 pamphlets, 15,000 volumes of periodicals and 15,000
maps and technical drawings. Its resources include rare
books, official publications, unit histories, journals, maps and
much fascinating printed ephemera such as aerial
propaganda leaflets, prisoner of war material, pamphlets,
and miscellanea. The department is the best starting point
for visitors interested in tracing family history. The Museum
does not hold individual service records but can help in
a general way.

The Sound Archive is a pioneer in the field of oral history.
It now holds some 35,000 hours of interviews and
recordings and offers the researcher a huge array of
experience to draw on. Coverage has been built up by
topic and selection influenced by the 'race against time' to
record reminiscences before it is too late. There are special
collections on particular themes such as the Spanish Civil
War and the Holocaust.

For Further Information ask for the free booklet:
The Collections: An Access Guide.

The National Inventory of War Memorials is an
information-gathering project. A database is being
created of all known war memorials in the UK, estimated
at between 50,000 and 60,000.

GENERAL INFORMATION

Education Service

The Museum's new Education Centre provides excellent facilities for a wide range of activities including talks, study sessions, drama, art, films and sixth form conferences on the two world wars, the Holocaust and conflict since 1945. Please write to the Head of Education for further details

Mailing List

For free up-to-date information about exhibitions and events write to the Head of Marketing and Visitor Services

Facilities for Disabled Visitors

There is wheelchair access into and through all museum galleries. Tickets can be pre-booked and parking arranged by appointment.
Telephone 020 7416 5397 (office hours)

Friends of the Imperial War Museum

Membership benefits include special events, a magazine and free admission to all Imperial War Museum sites. For further information telephone 020 7416 5255 (office hours)

Mail Order

For details of general and educational publications and other merchandise which can be supplied world-wide visit www.iwm.org.uk or telephone 01223 835000 x245 (office hours)

Donations and Legacies

The Museum welcomes donations and legacies from members of the public wishing to support its work. For information write to the Secretary or visit www.iwm.org.uk

Hospitality and Conferences

For facilities and hire charges telephone 020 7416 5394 (office hours)

Comments and Suggestions

Suggestions for improving our service are welcomed Please write to the Visitor Services Officer

Opening Hours

Open daily from 10.00am to 6.00pm
Closed 24, 25, 26 December
Access for Study: weekdays 10.00am to 5.00pm
Saturday Study Service: Documents and Printed Books only

The Holocaust Exhibition

To be sure of admission please book in advance on 020 7416 5439. 10.00am to 6.00pm

Admission Charges

Please telephone for current ticket prices
Children and senior citizens free
Discounts for groups, students, disabled and unemployed
Free for all after 4.30pm

General Enquiries and What's On Information

24-hour recorded information 09001 600140
All other enquiries 020 7416 5000 Fax 020 7416 5374
Web-site: www.iwm.org.uk
Imperial War Museum, Lambeth Road, London SE1 6HZ

IMPERIAL WAR MUSEUM

Cabinet War Rooms

Visit the warren of rooms that lie in the basement of a government building in Westminster. They served as the nerve centre of Churchill's government during the fight against the Nazis and are preserved just as they were in the Second World War.

Cabinet War Rooms, Clive Steps, King Charles Street, London SW1A 2AQ
Information 020 7939 6961 www.iwm.org.uk

HMS *Belfast*

Europe's last surviving big-gun armoured warship of the Second World War is permanently moored opposite the Tower of London. There are seven decks of exciting exhibition space to explore.

HMS *Belfast*, Morgans Lane, Tooley Street, London SE1 2JH
Information 020 7407 6434 www.iwm.org.uk

IWM Duxford

This former RAF Battle of Britain Fighter station now houses the finest collection of historic military and civil aircraft in the country, from the legendary Spitfire to the supersonic Concorde. See the stunning new American Air Museum and experience history in the air at Duxford's air shows.

IWM Duxford near Cambridge CB2 4QR
Information 01223 835000 www.iwm.org.uk

All sites are open daily except for 24, 25 and 26 December

Imperial War Museum - North

This major new museum will open in Trafford in 2002.

For further information 020 7416 5415 www.iwm.org.uk

IMPERIAL WAR MUSEUM - NORTH

The Central Map Room, Cabinet War Rooms

HMS Belfast at her moorings opposite the Tower of London

The American Air Museum

ISBN 1-901623-23-8

9 781901 623239 >